JUMBO JETS

Aaron Carr

LET'S READ AV² BY WEIGL™
ADDED VALUE • AUDIO VISUAL

Go to **www.av2books.com**, and enter this book's unique code.

BOOK CODE

N516678

AV² by Weigl brings you media enhanced books that support active learning.

AV² provides enriched content that supplements and complements this book. Weigl's AV² books strive to create inspired learning and engage young minds in a total learning experience.

Your AV² Media Enhanced books come alive with...

Audio
Listen to sections of the book read aloud.

Video
Watch informative video clips.

Embedded Weblinks
Gain additional information for research.

Try This!
Complete activities and hands-on experiments.

Key Words
Study vocabulary, and complete a matching word activity.

Quizzes
Test your knowledge.

Slide Show
View images and captions, and prepare a presentation.

... and much, much more!

Published by AV² by Weigl
350 5th Avenue, 59th Floor
New York, NY 10118
Website: www.av2books.com   www.weigl.com

Library of Congress Control Number: 2013936157
ISBN 978-1-62127-378-3 (hardcover)
ISBN 978-1-62127-384-4 (softcover)

Printed in the United States of America in North Mankato, Minnesota
1 2 3 4 5 6 7 8 9 0 17 16 15 14 13

052013
WEP040413

Project Coordinator: Aaron Carr   Art Director: Terry Paulhus

Weigl acknowledges Getty Images as the primary image supplier for this title.

JNF
629.133
CARR

JUMBO JETS

CONTENTS

Jumbo jets are big machines.
They fly people all over the world.

5

Jumbo jets can be different sizes. One of the biggest jumbo jets can seat 853 people.

Some jumbo jets are used to carry goods. The biggest jumbo jet can carry more than 550,000 pounds of goods.

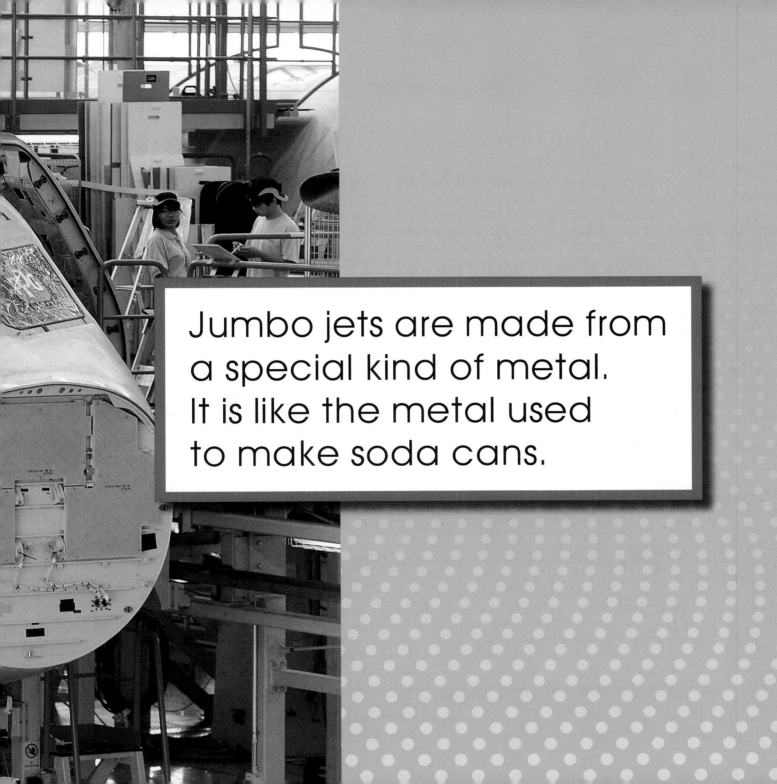

Jumbo jets are made from a special kind of metal. It is like the metal used to make soda cans.

Jumbo jets can fly very far. Some jumbo jets can fly more than 10,000 miles without landing.

Jumbo jets can fly more than 600 miles an hour.

Jumbo jets use special wheels to take off and land. The wheels are pulled inside the jet when it is flying.

Jumbo jets have a room
called the flight deck.
There are hundreds of lights
and buttons on the flight deck.

This is where the pilots
fly the plane.

17

The president of the United States flies in a special jumbo jet. It is called Air Force One.

Air Force One can refill its fuel tank while flying.

aner. Quieter. Smarter.

Jumbo jets are tested to make sure they are safe to fly. They go through 1,200 hours of test flying.

Pilots must spend years flying smaller planes before they can fly jumbo jets.

JUMBO JET FACTS

These pages provide more detail about the interesting facts found in the book. They are intended to be used by adults as a learning support to help young readers round out their knowledge of each machine featured in the *Mighty Machines* series.

Pages 4–5

Jumbo jets are big machines. They are the biggest airplanes in the world. Jumbo jets are also called wide-bodied aircraft. This is because they have three rows of seats and two aisles. The name 'jumbo jet' was first applied to the Boeing 747, but it has since become a common name for all wide-bodied aircraft.

Pages 6–7

Jumbo Jets can be different sizes. The first Boeing 747 could carry 490 people. Today, jumbo jets can carry a wide range of passengers and cargo, depending on the needs of the airline. Some jumbo jets carry as few as 200 people. The world's biggest passenger jumbo jet is the Airbus A380. This huge aircraft can seat up to 853 people.

Pages 8–9

Jumbo jets are also used to carry goods. Not all jumbo jets are made for carrying people. Some jumbo jets are designed to carry cargo. They are called freighters. These jumbo jets are used to transport goods all over the world. The world's largest jumbo jet is the Antonov An-225. This massive machine is almost as long as a football field and can carry 551,150 pounds (250,000 kilograms) of cargo.

Pages 10–11

Jumbo jets are made from a special kind of metal. Most jumbo jets are made from high-strength aluminum. Soda cans are also made from aluminum. This strong, light-weight metal helps keep these massive jets from becoming too heavy. The Airbus A380 is 16.5 tons (15 metric tons) lighter than it would be if it were made entirely of steel.

Jumbo jets can fly very far. Jumbo jets use as many as six huge jet engines to provide enough force to lift off the ground. These gigantic airplanes can fly up to 40,000 feet (12,192 meters) above the ground. Flying so high helps jumbo jets complete very long-distance flights. At that height, the air is thinner so the engines do not have to work as hard. The Boeing 777-200LR can fly 10,800 miles (17,380 km) without stopping.

Jumbo jets use special wheels to take off and land. A fully loaded Airbus A380 can weigh more than 1 million pounds (454,000 kg). For such a big machine to land and take off safely, it has to use special kinds of wheels, or landing gear. The Boeing 747-400 has 18 landing gear wheels. They are placed in groups of two or four along the length of the plane, including under each wing, under the body, and under the nose.

Jumbo jets have a room called a flight deck. The pilot and copilot fly the plane from the flight deck, or cockpit. The flight deck is located at the front of the plane. The walls and ceiling of the flight deck are covered in lights, buttons, switches, and gauges. These instruments allow pilots to control the plane. Many jumbo jets have a HUD, or head-up display, that allows pilots to see important information displayed on a transparent screen that sits in front of the windshield.

The president of the United States flies in a special jumbo jet. Technically, any U.S. Air Force aircraft carrying the president is called Air Force One. However, the name usually applies to one of two identical Boeing 747-200B jumbo jets. Both jets are kept at Andrews Air Force Base near Washington, D.C. The jets have special equipment designed to keep them safe in the event of a nuclear explosion. They can also refuel in mid-air, which allows them to fly to any place around the world.

Jumbo jets are tested to make sure they are safe to fly. Flying on a jumbo jet is one of the safest ways to travel. Of all aircraft operating today, the Airbus A340 and Boeing 777 have two of the best safety records. Airbus puts its jumbo jets through about 1,200 hours of test flights before they are cleared for regular use.

KEY WORDS

Research has shown that as much as 65 percent of all written material published in English is made up of 300 words. These 300 words cannot be taught using pictures or learned by sounding them out. They must be recognized by sight. This book contains 54 common sight words to help young readers improve their reading fluency and comprehension. This book also teaches young readers several important content words, such as proper nouns. These words are paired with pictures to aid in learning and improve understanding.

Page	Sight Words First Appearance	Page	Content Words First Appearance
4	all, are, big, over, people, the, they, world	4	jumbo jets, machines
7	be, can, different, of, one	7	sizes
9	carry, goods, more, some, than, to, used	9	pounds
11	a, from, kind, like, made, make, is, it	11	metal, soda cans
12	an, far, miles, very, without	12	hour
15	and, land, off, take, when	15	jet, wheels
16	called, have, is, lights, on, there, this, where	16	buttons, flight deck, pilots, plane, room
18	in	18	Air Force One, president, United States
19	its, while	19	fuel tank
21	before, go, must, through, years	21	test flying

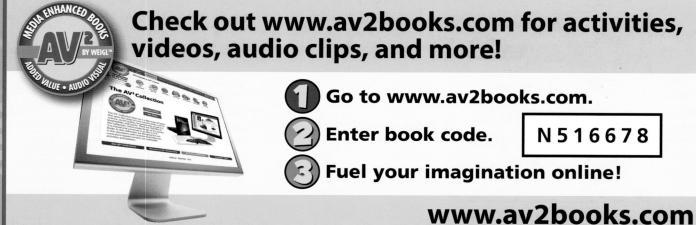